I Am The Title

Michael Day

Front Porch History
2013

I dedicate this work to humanity

Contents

I wrote this for no one,
except for you

Life, Noted

The wind was magnificent, pushing objects from rest, creating a world of altered arrangements. Sometimes I can hear his voice on winds like this, whispering fragile into the rush around my ears.

My porch had seen many a year, with and without Chris. We watched silhouettes of still things until they came to life. He had always been there, dancing between the shadows.

Chris, when his heart still beat, was rarely present. He was not a religious man. He was a skeptic of all things organized. Institutions, he claimed, collectively disenfranchise the individual. He drifted between his darkroom and his desk. Words and photos, he said, have varying layers of complexity. Within those layers are truth.

Chris could not live on the surface. He eloquently moved through trapdoor thoughts and away from the front stage, favoring observation and theory from behind the curtain. I wish I saw what he knew.

Like many an artist, Chris ended his life abruptly. I had a lover's pang of prescient sorrow on the train back home. Standing opposite him, I saw his last tears leave him. I inhaled his breath as he pushed through the security guard's hold. I caressed the back of his neck as he crossed his arms and let gravity take him to the stone. The impact, stole me. The train arrived and Chris was gone.

Now I sit, sipping his scotch, and listening to Dylan. The world passes in a slow and steady urgency. A guff of wind works its way through me, knocking out my cigarette. As I reach for my lighter, Chris exhales and my fingers find an envelope.

My Dearest Natalie,

When the sun-bleached Earth turns, it speaks in hushed silence. I look for the beacon, heart sparked sentiments of learned love, gratitude, and calm. To this, I submit myself once again, having learned the deceits of death and conquered nothing. With unflinching desire I grasp what eludes.

Ghosts from a darkened age cling to my shell, rapping at my coffin with infinite indifference. I choose life, my dearest Natalie.

Godspeed,

Christopher

The final words wrinkle mangled and mashed in my hands, tear soaked and heart broke. I placed the note on the table next to me, removed a rock from Chris's garden and weighed it down.

I returned to our porch, slowly rocking in my chair. The sun began to set, bringing layers of darkness and loss, and the promise.

The promise of truth.

Barbato

It's a long, Long Island,
when trading breaths for
euphoria, and
slipping sideways, towards
inward.

I can feel John, in
the heavy, thick
molecules, settling
dusts of many, and
the collapsing lift of all forms.

I can smell John,
in the absence of summer,
leaves carrying his scent, in
the early approach to the,
fall.

I can see John, sick and struggling,
flashing
cloudy eyes,
from a storm swept brain.

I can hear John,
ghosts escaping in
mangled muffled battles. He
was listening
for colors, in
a black and white world. It's a long, Long Island,

when trading breaths for
euphoria, and
slipping sideways,
towards inward.

The Drugs on War

Merchants of hope slide between the shadows, acquainting themselves with the deep despair of acquisition. Partake in us. We offer the resolution, mouth their eyes. Donte's currency loses itself in their palms and his hand gathers hope. Silently they creep beneath their shadows into the underbelly.

Donte returns to his apartment and sits in his favorite chair, toying with the bag of dope. The chemical circle refuses to be broken. They stand with their arms interlocked in solidarity, refusing to acknowledge their obtrusiveness. The manifestation of their insistence and committed resolve levies its powerful purpose on Donte's physical being. Their origins are unknown, yet he finds just cause in acquainting them with what he holds dear. Behind the mask, Donte understands the severity of his actions, but acquiesces in the name of ignorance. He allows the chemicals to molest his better nature and toy with the darkest depths of his detachment.

Scale is reduced and the influx of chemicals rushes Donte's blood stream, searching for a way to rob him of reality. The ugliest part is his division from the whole and the comfort he finds in doing so. On cold winter nights Donte would drape himself with his fears, and his frosty breath would push the ghosts from his core. He is one with those agents of change.

Perhaps it is better here.

How would he know otherwise? Donte only knew of despair and the crumbling remains of what was once fair and just. The dead cold of the winter has vanished and the cold dead of the other seasons has traded their existence for something greater through that dope. Slowly slips the sorrow of his corner.

The tears of the woman on the roof are dancing back from

the concrete, replacing themselves where they belong. The flesh, stolen by bullets, reassembles itself. The car is flying back down the street in reverse and the child is no longer transfixed by the headlights aimed at her bones. The thought fails to gestate, therefore removing its vile delivery, and he is saved from the razor.

Donte juggles the remainder of the baggie and its contents, shifting it from one opportunity it another. His forearm twitches in anticipation. He imagines the shrieks of fiends if the powder met the water. They are twisting and contorting their fears of becoming sick, failing to realize that the sickness has become them. Chance knows no opponent stronger than certainty, and Donte was certain that chance is dead.

Donte removes himself from the arm chair and stretches his body. He opens the front door and walks into sunshine.

Building 65

Hallowed halls echo memories of those, that
slide between
Just and Right.

Those with
calculated indifferences
are borne,
of passionate lives lost.

Their shadows are
constructed from
a different type of darkness,
a different sort of vacant.

Supposing these souls,
recover,
Recovery emulated,
by those to be recovered and
once, another left to be discovered
feels found.

Dilated speak.
Sleep. Sing. Bring new
life.
Light.
Bright.

Dream safe.
Dream right.
Speak, easy song
in lonesome crowded space.

Sift
through needle less nights.
Fall up from the liquor,
withdrawn.
Sneeze cough coke,
money
unfolded and
safe.

Blood shot battered
and bruised. Liver
left normal, and
shocked into humanity,
shocked into discourse.

Normal needed
now,
and rest.

Civil Whites

Battle tested gentlemen creatively maneuver their worlds without war on stoops steeped in history of a different sort. Infants bounce from one lap to another, tragic trajectories trickling from the corner of their young lips, dribbling insecurities not yet known.

Seasons pass indiscriminately onward. The frigid hard stare of winter has met its match. Cracked lips and bleeding hearts yearn for summer justice, but live in the shadows of winter warfare. Transformed corners adopt different shades of color at shallow speeds. Those on the cooperative corners cite green as causation, but the color responsible for this situation is blinding.

Property owners perched from rooftops miles away marvel at the misinformation. Later, maps will be drawn with red lines, removing culture from the soldiers and opportunity from their children. Twisted faces sing ignorance and children cry themselves to poor.

The spring brings nothing. Corners still crumple under the weight of injustice. Memories are boarded up until forever. Streetlights dim to the color of despair and abandon blocks harbor screams for their lost patrons.

The rain ceases and the summer befalls the gentlemen. It's a light blue massacre in 1968 Chicago. Direct your attention to the Chicago 7, but ignore the thousands, if not hundreds of thousands, of Chicagoans still fighting. Anti-war protests are held for a visible war, but there will not be any demonstrations for the war the gentlemen faced.

One rock from the yard.
One brick from the home.
One nail from the wall.

Say goodbye to your history. Say goodbye to your community. Chicago owns it now.

Synonymous

Never again will the loud, color the trees, whispering the stories of winters past. They have been raped from their land.

Brilliant, decayed leaves tell stories of generations lost, generations found.

The strength of their trunks are emblematic of the nations they once were home to but, just as nations fall, so have they.

Roots, entangled with other systems, exemplify the life complexities that we, as humans, must embrace. They have been stripped from insects, the soil, and water as we will be stripped from neighbors, land, and our lives.

Anthony thinks of this as he attaches the rope, swings to his tree and enjoys what will

certainly come to an end.

Faith Departed

Re: Soul #312,513,2568

Dear God,

Dear God. Let this letter serve as my formal resignation and as a binding agreement, absolving me from any commitments previously honored, i.e. praying, fear, unflinching loyalty to an Orwellian big brother, etc. The time has come for me to retire my faith and push past servitude. I have been to your brother's hell and my brother's hell and,

I have seen saviors selling your heaven on the corner of 125th and Morningside. In Basra I found you within the veils and in the distance between bullets around Mesopotamia. Yesterday I heard you between the lyrics of Marley and Cash. One time, I tasted you in saffron ice-cream in Tehrangeles and the last time I touched you was in the folds of Aboriginal skin. I find you everywhere except where you claim to be.

Therefore, it is with regret that I must inform you that your services are no longer needed. If this offends, then it only serves as an offense to myself and that, I can live with.

Godspeed,

Your heathen

Montauk

Nathan is dead. A once bright flicker in Julie's womb, is now no more. Now I sleep. I slept yesterday, all day. I slept into today, and Julie will likely find me asleep well into tomorrow.

So I dream, and dreamt, and will till I am done. Julie is calling me. I hear her through the fuzzy and the blurry. "Miguel, wake my love." In a trailing slur of bumbled vocabulary I answer her. "Not yet. I just got to the good part."

Dripped darkness and light and then, a light in the dark. Silouhettes. Then, movement of shadows float towards me. Closer. Closer. Closer. Then, far.

I am grasping for something distant. The object is not so remote that it is removed from my field of vision, but not close enough for me to ascertain its importance. The only thing that is definitive is that I want it. For a fleeting fortunate moment my vision corrects itself and the object becomes lucid. Nathan. He is calling to me, beckoning me to move closer. I exhaust my strength and collapse with my efforts.

Waking on the deck of our summer home in Montauk, Julie hovers over me, placing a needle to a record. Our world is consumed by Chopin. I watch as Nathan's eardrums adapt to the new sound. Those wondrous instruments move him to motion. We dance together and fall into a tired heap on the deck. A short while later I am walking down our steps, feeling the wood on my feet. Nathan cries, his tiny foot the victim of a splinter. I console him and the tears subside.

The wood meets the sand and Nathan follows me over the crest. As the ocean becomes visible, I am consumed. Nathan, jaw agape, cannot construct a sentence to explain what is being experienced. I glance down at those eyes. His calculating cameras are taking snapshots of this newly discovered piece of his universe and working with the clarity that is robbed from us as we age. Nathan and I continue on and find a small boardwalk close to the water. After walking for a good while, Nathan tugs at my shirt, begging for some type of confection being sold. I concede and watch as his taste buds react. He delights in the ecstasy that is sugar and begins to run ahead of me in youthful jubilance.

Suddenly, Nathan is being yanked by shadows and I am grasping

Screaming.
Crying.
Yelling.
Running.
Leaping.
Falling.
Failing.

My arms are outstretched as my body meets the ground.
All my hands find are sand, and Julie.

Rejected Recourse

Dear Kind Master of Educationialism,

Please give me a moment of your endowment coddling time.

I am a spitfire intellectual breathing the dreams of dignified discourse. I mock your halls in modest respect and will dance from head to head on your uselessly irrelevant stone representations of dead history. Flaunting obscure tastes in reprehensible forms of non-elitist film and theater, I plan to spoil the minds of young yacht frequenters. Clubbed country insurrection will baffle suburbanite slang.

With passionate gusto I will rip the symbols of ensemble imperialism from your student's polo's and burn them with the retinas of the less clothed. Slamming stoned stanzas against stories of gifted degrees and family exchanged property, I will glowingly fascinate the student body with my ghetto fabulous tales, sparing no details for the bubbled students.

Stoically, I will storm the student council and electrify the legislative bodies with cries for civility for the poverty philanthropist collective. Have they no voice? This malicious mockery of the legislative process will not stand. A call for the creation of a Green Republican Communist Theocracy will resound throughout the halls of frivolous golf course banter.

Please, kind sir, consider me for admission to the School of Disenchanted Elitist School Applicants for a lofty pursuit of a Master's in Debauchery.

This is what I can bring to you King Squire of Intellect.

Sincerely not,

THE STUDENT

War Wrinkled

In his wrinkles,
I see Viet Nam. Muscle
contortions are memories
in, the fold of his
skin.

Lived lost souls, collapse
when the frown
retreats. Stone
cold horrors, hide
for a while.

He holds a skull
beside him. Empty
eye socket dreams, are
singed with nocturnal
fires, but dressed in
mourning dew.

The skull sings
selfish, crying
for flesh escaped.

Eyes elicit inquiry. They
speak of actions flame
forged, yet
he smiles
in dance,
with indifferent shrugs
and, makes
light

of all things heavy.

The frown returns and,
there we were.

Punkdrose

Through the window I see a lone vacant bar stool. Embrace me, it beckons, deceitfully altering its height to arrange my placement on it. My hands, clasped in mocked reverence, rest on the wood grain. I disentangle my fingers and slide my palm along the wood, collecting the stories of those who have sat where I now sit. Forged relationships and shattered hearts found their ways in the dull drain of cells through liquid. The bottles, with their strategically marketed colors and images wreak havoc on the decision making process. Liquid ambivalence drips from the taps as the bartenders inquiry delivers me to the present.

One Johnny Walker Blue. One Macallan. One Pacifico. Three regrets. Straight up. Sip, flinch, squirm, shutter, jolt. Knock it back. My blood is thinning and my thoughts are racing.

I am dismantling my atoms with a voraciousness not seen since the gathering of them. This shell needs to be cast aside in defiance and the world must see my truth. The masses must be intoxicated by the release of those intangible feelings only realized through the deconstruction of the physical form. Sleep well tonight because tomorrow you will take ownership of my thoughts. Town by town. City by City. Person by person. What was once elusive inquisitiveness will now be accessible and impossible to ignore. Collectively, this nation will feel and see and cry and struggle and squirm. This is my gift to us. No thank you necessary. The bartender approaches.

One Johnny Walker Black, straight up. Forgo the ice and the de-masculinization that the cubes represent. I am a man. I take my liquor straight. The floor accepts my gait failure with indifference.

A splash of light and my iris meets reality. My vision is blurry, but it soon becomes apparent that my body must become acclimated to a medical setting. A burly man looms above me, minimizing my stature to helplessness, and begins to ask foggy questions. The words and sentences are disjointed. Appear. Life. Suicide. 1.8. BAC. Family. A needle protrudes my vein and the scrambled words collect in structured coherent thoughts. "Are you thinking of taking your own life," asks the doctor. "Where," I ask inquisitively. He cocks his head in confusion, searching for a response. Instead, he closes the curtain and walks away. Another injection and I am floating. Floating above the hospital. Floating about Manhattan. Floating above floating. I have moved into a different place with a different space and the words slip slowly towards coherence.

Numbers must be made to assume a human characteristic. Repeatedly, attempts are made to use numbers to deliver a nation, a group, or a people to an empirically grounded answer to questions concerned with the progress or sustainment of the human condition, be it fruitful or nefarious. They become a part of the human experience and can no longer be identified as being merely inanimate objects used to relay information. In their use, they move into a realm that is associated with the connection of all things, living or not. This realm is where humanity rests, eagerly anticipating answers to obvious questions.

Solitarily, numbers, on the tips of pens of those in academia remain numbers, used correctly or incorrectly to advance or devolve the human condition. In consideration of the impact that mathematics has had on both the civilized world and communities lacking civility alike, perhaps their utility and contributions to the human condition should be re-evaluated and prescribed a status stronger than a mere association to text.

"Is that so? Numbers? Yeah. Let's go ahead and beginning categorizing your belongings son. Oh, and for the record, Christopher Hitchens cannot be on your visitor list. I am sorry to tell you that he passed some time ago." A giant Lenny of a man placed his hand on my sunken shoulder. "Shoes are fine, but I need you to remove the laces." One backpack, check. One cell phone and a charger, check. One journal, check. Sorry my man, but you cannot keep the pen. One Walt Whitman copy of Leaves of Grass, check. One pair of sunglasses, check. Okay, all of your stuff will be safe with me. Let's get you to your bed, bud."

No lock. No door. No shower door. Four beds. Four screw-ups. Government issued soap, deodorant, tooth brush, tooth paste, and a bucket for water.

The door to my new space was ajar, a small amount of light emanating into the callously cold hallway from a single red bulb. Two beds were adjacent to one another on each side of the room, creating a space discomfortingly close enough to create mocked intimacy, yet far enough to create confusion. I stepped into the light as a man, once slumbered, raised his head in curiosity. The query was curt and he returned to his state of detachment. Lenny left me to my new environment and closed the door that never was.

Humanist Abomination-Juxstapositional Insurgency

Prone position fixed, I
scope soft sympathetic
signatures.

Chopper drops fast
rope fanatics, with
harmony shelled
casings, erupting
into sunsets, and slowly leaking humanity
into, the stars.

Convoy stricken
ripe rippled, improvised
empathetic determination
moves
through all.

Array of stark struck
colors, through
rocket propelled
generosity, aimed
at the one, that
equals all.

Shadow soldiers
slit ignorance, in

the halls of
humanity.

Watching.
Waiting.
Evolving.

Sunrise surrogates step
beyond archaic
anthems, moving
towards the path
followed by
one.

Social Worked

Writer met with social worker at bedside to assess and discuss general malaise with the Veterans Administration (VA) hospital system. Social worker presented as alert and oriented x's three, but exhibited symptoms representative of Axis 1 disorders, possibly major depressive disorder or a social anxiety disorder. Writer recommends that the medical team order a psychiatric evaluation. Social worker states that he was "driven to enter the field of social work in an attempt to balance out the inconsistencies between human dignity and how the system has been designed to treat humans."

Social worker resides in a studio apartment in Manhattan by himself. Most recent performance appraisal provided to writer suggests that social worker currently suffers from a variety of substance abuse issues. When asked if social worker would like to be referred to an inpatient or outpatient substance abuse rehabilitation program social worker replied "Hell, no. how would I kill the countless horrendous memories of traumas that I hear or witness every day?"

Social worker has some type of government insurance that covers just enough to dwindle social worker's meager paycheck to nothing. Social worker stated, "What the heck, we get paid very little for the work that we do?" Writer attempted to console social worker by informing him that there are other occupations that received far less money; such as janitors and people who work at fast food restaurants. Social worker responded by stating, "Do they have a Master's Degree?" Writer unable to provide a suitable response that would appropriately address social worker's inquiry.

Prior to being admitted to the VA, the social worker was not in receipt on any skilled or non-skilled nursing services.

Social worker however, reports a steady decline in his ability to verbally articulate his inability to offer sufficient services for housing, home care, or substance abuse rehabilitation services to veterans because of limited resources and declining interest in achieving optimal health performance measures from the hospital administration. Social worker states that, "I am slowly losing the ability to explain to veterans what I cannot offer them." Writer will recommend that medical team put in a speech therapist consult.

Plan:

Writer will refer social worker to three month outpatient social work rehabilitation course and recommend placement in an intentionally ambiguous federal language speech pathology seminar. Writer will continue to address any additional issues that may arise prior to discharge of social worker.

bOOm

It began with a click.

Falling up from the pavement,
I pause.

> Violence is of an unknown etiology. Perhaps originating from one of those rules forged through decades of ignorant wisdom.
>
> Or, a stagnated cultural covenant, oblivious to the advancement of our species and our environment.
>
> Maybe, a lone archaic anthem, passed through bloodlines.
>
> Possibly, a misplaced ideal, wrapped in a web of misinformation.

> Lip lashed scoldings are fired in rapid rhythm. Your fault. My Fault. Our fault. Their fault. Heads hang in confused complicity. Even the children are soundless. Tooth dust paints the sidewalk as genetic markers spill across the grass.

On both knees now, flesh
grinding against grit and love escaping through gasps,

I see. Then, CLICK.

Purple

Undocumented aborted
fetuses, rally for
community organized
trickle-down voter fraud.
Human being dinosaurs
evolve science books into
monkeys, and
stem celled climates drain resources in
offshore oil sweatshops.

Outsourced Marxist birth
certificates, collect
in Mosques built by free
market,
patriots.

Liberty loving death
panels, burn Tea Party food
stamp flags, at anti-Medicare
gun rallies.

Collective Unitarians enjoy
cups of
free trade socialism at,
gay marriage war crime
tribunals.

The middle becomes nowhere,
The Left becomes Right,
The Right is unknown and,

All
I
see,

is purple.

Proximity

I should have told you that tomorrow,
is not nearly as close, as
yesterday was.

That,
our sunsets would suspend, and
splendid notes listened to on a deeply stained
deck, would only be celebrate by one set of ears.

That,
those years held reverently,
would be dismissed as, forgotten memories,
pushed into boxes of photos in the corner
of your mind. Or, that the caress felt on

your face, would soon be no more than
wind and rain, dancing across your flesh.

I should have told you that,
as the death of life,
fell from your womb, so
would I,
slip from your presence. And that us, could only

be us,
for time less acceptable than,
you could have known.

Ascended Aesthetics

It was late December. Normally Carlos would have ridden his bike home, but it was a frozen 30 degrees and he was ill equipped for the weather. He locked his bike up for the night and hopped the uptown 6 train at 14th street. Immediately Carlos regretted his decision, having failed to notice the rush hour push. At 23rd street a rare opportunity presented itself as a sitting young man he was standing in front of gave the customary seat vacation nod. Carlos checked his periphery for ladies without seats. Seeing none, he obliged, promising to return the favor to another, one day. He scanned what he could with his limited field of vision, but was met with crotches and awkward eyes. The train's momentum jostled passengers and belongings, creating a maze of space that Carlos diligently navigated with his eyes. She appeared between a newspaper and a shoulder. Then he found her between a backpack and curly hair. Each shift of the passengers and their belongings brought a shift in Carlos's eyes. He scanned and hoped and maneuvered space, hoping for a glimpse.

She was sultry sexy. Her purple peat coat, adorned with a yellow peace pin, was slung over her arm. She was exotic, the type of person that always managed to elude the guesses you thought may be correct. Her face was flawlessly symmetrical with pouty lips and doe eyes. Her dimples became well highlighted as she smiled with perfectly aligned teeth and said excuse me to riders brushing past her to exit the train. Her long dark hair bounced off her shoulders. The strands were ferociously black.

The crowd around her thinned as the train raced further Uptown. Carlos could now see her neck and the lime blue blouse she wore. A trickle of subway sweat danced down her neck towards her breasts. Three stops later her midsection became visible. Her flat stomach tensed and her muscles tightened with sudden jolts of the train. An ancient relic hung from her belly button, adding intensity to her mystique. This pinnacle of genetics had gathered quite the audience from 14th street to 86th street.

As the train approached the 96th street station, the riders blocking his view of her, in her entirety, prepared to depart. Carlos followed her magnificent hair and the curve of her body down past her midsection and stopped. She was wearing a lovely earth toned skirt with baby blue spirals wrapping around part of her thighs and her backside. Beneath those spirals were two legs, severely burned.

Carlos's eyes shifted around the train, observing the other men who hand fancied her for the last 82 streets. They had turned their heads from her, noticeably disgusted. The skirt was arguably too high for someone afflicted with such aesthetic imperfection. She glanced around the train and noticed the shift in attention. Her eyes met Carlos's as he began to stand and approach her. The conductor announced the train arrival at his stop, 103rd street. He looked at the doors as they closed and, returned his attention to her, and said "that was my stop." "You should have gone like they usually do," she said in an indistinguishable accent. Carlos looked deep into those doe eyes.

He saw the fire capture her legs as she tried to run from that monster. Carlos tried to understand the difficulty in the decision that she made before she left her home this morning. She had chosen a skirt on a cold day.

Carlos moved within an inch of her face. Her breath met his and he felt the heat from her body. He felt the vibrations and vibes and energy and truth.

The conductor announced the train's arrival at 110th street.

Carlos took hold of her hand. He turned towards the doors, and then back towards her gaze. "This is our stop" he said.

Lose Lose

Sweat is pouring down her neck. This is Brooklyn in July. The stifling heat crowds Allison's discomfort. Her agency does not have air conditioning and, thankfully, today she will journey to another neighborhood. Her supervisor has asked her to present a youth program to a group of high school students. She steps off the train and observes. There are substantially more vacant stores than open ones. There are more vacant homes than occupied. More despair than repair creates the converse of picturesque. Before her is a model of the devolution of the forgotten corners of this country. Young children dash through an open hydrant, oblivious to their plight and savoring those small moments of happiness as only children and a handful of adults know how. This is a celebration of life in decay.

Allison delivers her message to a gym filled with youth. She tells them of a world stripped of their own experiences. Allison paints a canvas of life much larger than their individual needs and wants. She invites them to be consumed and consume alike, the wondrous nature of the unknown. She challenges them to bring more to this world than they now know they can. A large number of students are receptive to what the program can offer them. Allison returns to her neighborhood with a list of contacts and a smile. She walks into the sweltering office and notices a different severity in the frowns that are commonplace at my agency. Project funding has been severed to make room for more programs that will be cut in the future to make more room for programs that will be cut in the future. Allison stares at her list of contacts. They are meaningless now.

A program participant stumbles into the office and is bleeding profusely from his face. He was beaten on the street for his stipend check. No trouble, until now. His eyes, once wide to prospects and possibilities, are now confused pupils, narrowed from the hyper vigilance often exhibited by the accosted. His frown formed that day, shaping his face for the rest of his short life.

Allison tosses her contact list into the wastebasket and closes her door.

Rational Religion

Three walls in Anthony's four cornered room share a common tranquility of barrenness. It makes the meticulously centered portrait of Richard Dawkins on the fourth wall an object of remarkable significance. Anthony rests on his bed and becomes mesmerized with the portrait all over again. Slowly he removes himself from the covers and kneels beside his bed.

Glancing at Dawkins he places his elbows on his blankets and clasps his hands in reverence. Separating the intent from the symbolism, Anthony says a brief prayer, seeking a day of thoughts inspired by logical thinking and rational choices. He does this every day, religiously.

Anthony grabs his journal and throws it in his bag, preparing for a day of inquiry, and pauses to observe his surroundings. He should be blessed. He should be humbled by the simplicity of his room. Authors, remarkable, unremarkable, and absurd, line Anthony's bookshelf. His clothes are scattered along my floor, next to his mattress. Anthony is barely living. He celebrates, however, in the simplistic nature of his possessions and environment; reserving complexity for his attempts to interpret the world and the streets of Manhattan. Photos line the periphery of Anthony's one sacred possession, his desk. Anthony's mother is holding her husband tightly in one photo, attempting to compensate for the space lost over time.

He slams the door on his refuge and momentarily deliberates about returning to pray once more. Anthony moves reluctantly towards the bathroom to prepare for the day. Taking a deep breath, he exhales a small percentage of insecurities and leaves the bathroom for breakfast. The food in Anthony's refrigerator provides little sustenance and he departs his home feeling hungry for everything.

Rounding the corner, Anthony sees Pastor Sean standing at the steps of his sanctuary, looking weathered and charmed, gray hairs preaching experience. Passing the church, Anthony touches his index finger to the tip of his hat and Pastor Sean nods in recognition. "Found Jesus yet, my son?" Anthony grins and says, "Pastor Sean, I was not aware that you had lost him."

Anush

Some people have a way of collapsing the metaphysical bound-aries between nature and one's self. The softness of their breath moves the currents and molecules collapse and cooperate with the boisterousness of their eyes. Their voice commands the winds and their physical movements move stars. They hold our globe on a fingernail and transfix nature with their au-dacity. They keep things complete. They, without knowing, balance what must be balanced. It is with their heartbeats that the cyclic nature of all hums. Unimaginable darkness fills the void in their absence. Stars collapse and planets fall from ex-istence of imploded galaxies when they pass from this world. Clocks refuse constant motion for there is no justifiable cause for time to move forward. They are the beginning. They are the middle. They must be the end.

They are people's mothers, sisters, fathers, and lovers. To some they are not. For many, time remains stagnant and stars fail to illuminate their violent nights. They pass to another plane never knowing how the world might have been shown to them. They are the cocoon, abandoned for the sake of beauty. The majestic flight of the butterfly is made possible by those that will never see it.

I hold the photo in my hand. It captures the details of our world as we shared it with one another. We are standing on the beach in the photo, Anush and I. It is a cloudless day of sunshine and calm waves. Before the photo was snapped, she had exhaled and pushed the ferocious wind from the waves. She turned to me and spoke as I watched the sun burst through the clouds. Finishing her thought, Anush looked toward the sky and the rain retreated towards the clouds. Moments before my mother pressed the button to capture the photo, Anush yawns, and the clouds are pushed from our atmosphere.

The globe is resting on her fingertip and fortunately for me, I cannot fathom seeing what I see in any other way. When our days have passed and we sit idly in anticipation of the end, I will pull the photo from my pocket. It will be studied as we wonder what each other will do in the darkness when one of us passes from this world. I already know. When Anush closes her eyes the world will fall dark.

Skittles

Raymond acquiesced to the recommendations of his therapist until his daily dosage of normality resembled a packet of Skittles. Raymond's supply provided a pill for every pained problem. They were tiny servings of stability until his mind became acutely aware of the trick he had played on it. When his brain began to recognize his deceitful plan, resiliency became paramount and the memories fought past the medication.

Raymond was robbed early on. His father's torturous temperament tore through his self-esteem and declared war on his well-being. The end result was the creation of a level of insecurity so heinous in its severity that it made the good things worse and the best things bad. His father's words spread throughout each thought and destroyed any opportunity for them to exist. Raymond wished his dad had beaten him every day and left his ideas alone.

The mental terrorism was uniform from his father's recognition of his existence in this world, throughout adolescence, and toils in Raymond's thoughts of tomorrow. His father was, and continues to be a relentless thought monster that spent a better part of his life attempting to destroy what he created.

Raymond knew that his propensity to favor harmful solutions when faced with a quandary in life had origins far beyond his conscious understanding. There is only one piece of information that he knew definitively; my father made me, me. Perhaps with the help of his lady, his doctor, and his therapist he can pick up the pieces. Until then, Raymond has a one color cure for each concern.

Hysterical Documents

Declaration of Dependence

We hold these truths to be self-evident, that all men, not women, are created equal unless they are black, Latino, gay or the combination of any of the aforementioned, that they are endowed by a Creator, regardless if they believe in a Creator or not, with a couple of vague unalienable Rights, that among these are Life, Liberty and the pursuit of Happiness, for which a definition of each will be constructed by a small elite group of white males. That to secure these rights, Governments are instituted among Men, not women or minorities, deriving their just powers from the consent of the governed that we see fit to be defined as citizens.

Pledge of Resistance

I plead no allegiance to the flag of the United States of corporate interests and to something that slightly resembles a Republic, for which greed stands, a failed nation, with an occasional God, certainly divisible, for Liberty and Justice, but not for all.

This is wAR

I am shackled to this War.
It will not allow me to
leave and I am afraid I am
going to die alone because
who is going to want to be
with me in
side my head and dealing
with the horrible things
that I think about myself
and the world and I can't
stop crying and I don't
know what
will make it better I am
really scared that I am
going to die alone I don't
want money I don't want
power I don't want a nice
car or a house I just don't
want to die alone I can't
even type right now I am
crying so hard and I
thought
let it flow and
see what comes of it I am
not so sure this was a good
idea it hurts so bad snot
dripping from my face and
my eyes flooded with tears
and I don't care
I am just drooling and

crying and wondering if it
will end and if it does end
who will it end with they
say write about what you
know and I feel like I
don't know anything anymore
so how can I write I am
scared I will die a
lone in this dumb apartment
in a place where no one
ever comes and I just don't
feel like I have much
left in me like there is nothing
left inside I feel dead
already and numb and who
would want me like this and
who would
like me like this and who
would need me like this
This Is War and I want to
wake up and everything is
fine but everything is not
fine and I can't sleep
because of bills and I have
to work because of bills so
I will get up and just go
to work
and pretend that it is
okay
but it is not okay and
I need help
and I want to check in to
somewhere that can help me

but the bills bills bills
where will I live I have a
lease I need help but I
can't speak or listen or understand I hate
the way we
live I hate the way I live
I can't figure anything out
why is everything so
foreign to me
that is a horrible feeling
to have deep inside you
that only comes out when
someone provokes you or
you've had one too many or
you see that same look of
pain in a friend's eyes and
know exactly what they are
going through but you can't
do anything because you
can't even help yourself
and when the hugs don't
work anymore

whatisleftwhatisleftwhatisleft

My World, the Sheath

Insert me.

Rearrange the world's
atoms with contorting
twists or,
reconfigure our present,
with twisted
contortions.

Slide in, like you love me to.
Feel the warm,
flush flesh paradise,
spilling from humanity in a
manner, not so different
from how it was created.

Initiate that old aged
tension, of
where I do,
and do not belong.

You use me, cutting pain
through,
scars once cut before.

Sheath me or unleash me,
in pointless positioning,
as the worldscar bleeds,
warm histories
indefinitely.

Infinitesimal cuts ripple
through us, stabbing
soliloquies dead,
and removing voice, from
a loud world.

You secure me,
sleeping silently
on a bed on indifference,
connecting humanity, or
it's decimation,
to actions
not words.

Inside your room,
calculating consequences,
you sit in dank darkness.

In and out of light,
moves your face,
as the light swings
methodically.
With each passing of the light
across your face, you
protect me.

and

As the light passes,

and
darknesses consume the room,
you remove me, and
place me to your flesh.

Little cuts,
just to see the life,
slowly slipping

until the light no longer
illuminates,
the world.

Remove me.

City Breath

I flee my apartment, pushing past the people that create what I need. No longer can solitude be tolerated. I walk the streets of the city, appalled at the rampant consumerism, but consuming nonetheless. My consumption however, is not of a materialistic nature. I consume the lights; I consume the sights, both unknown dialects and known dialects alike. I consume the movements of the masses and consume their immobility in the same manner.

Everything that I have learned about my disorder leads me to believe that this is not the City for me. The chaos, they say, is toxic for the mind controlled by post-traumatic stress. The noise, the movements, and the ominous intensity of the density cloud my perception. I am hyper vigilant in my consumption and attempt to be aware of all, but concentrate on none. It is felt in my movement and I see my cumbrousness in the eyes of others. It is odd to think that I am but a microcosm of the momentum of the City. When I am not consuming the City I lay my head to rest on a cheap pillow on a cheap bed which rests on cheap wood inside a cheaply painted Manhattan room with an expensive price tag.

Mos Def resounds from my room into the valley of buildings. "Escucha la ciudad respirando." I listen and I can *feel* it. I can feel the City breathing. From my fire escape, I hang my feet over the edge and listen to the sounds of The City. The lights of a police helicopter rest heavy against the few spots of darkness. If you squint your eyes...I mean just barely keep them open... it looks like the lights emanating from the projects are the nerves of the City. The lights become little synapses firing, connecting all the buildings to one another to create one massive electrical charge. The City hums with a cyclic rhythm, inhaling and exhaling. My light emanating from my room is a synapse firing to someone looking across the way from the projects. I am part of the perpetual cycle and acknowledging such calms me. She knocks on my door and I breathe slowly.

We snuck onto the roof from the sixth floor, Monika and I. With a bottle of wine and blanket in hand, we laid on the roof, connecting the stars to our imaginations. We breathed air easily in our own space and then drew upon one another's breaths.

The hour draws late and Monika says farewell. It feels good to be good with that.

Acknowledgments

The completion of this work would have not been possible without the insight, watchful eyes, and dedicated time of Allison and Jeff Zitnak, Darice Johnston, Jennie Fischer, Evan Shinner, Liat Alon, Chris Lockamy, Ray Daniel Medina, Lovella Callica, Erica Leone, Marco Antonio y Laura Guzman, Remy Benoit, Paul M. Rodriguez, Paul Wasserman, Warrior Writers, Warrior Writers NYC, Seeing Here Now, the NYU Writing Workshop, and my mother, Patricia Edson. Thank you to all of my family and friends for unconditional support and encouragement.

www.ingramcontent.com/pod-product-compliance
Lightning Source LLC
Chambersburg PA
CBHW031333040426
42443CB00005B/329